# *SHATTERING YOUR STRONGHOLDS*

## The Workbook

# SHATTERING YOUR STRONGHOLDS

## The Workbook

by

Liberty S. Savard

**BRIDGE-LOGOS** *Publishers*

North Brunswick, New Jersey

**Shattering Your Strongholds Workbook**
by Liberty S. Savard
ISBN: 0-88270-736-1
Copyright©1997 by Liberty S. Savard.

Published by:
**BRIDGE-LOGOS** *Publishers*
North Brunswick Corporate Center
1300 Airport Road, Suite E
North Brunswick, NJ 08902-1700

For further information regarding books, workbooks, tapes, speaking engagements, and workshops, please contact:

Liberty Savard Ministries
P.O. Box 41260
Sacramento, CA 95841-0260

# Contents

# Introduction to Workbook

*"Jesus said, I will give you the keys of the kingdom of heaven; whatever you bind on earth will be bound in heaven, and whatever you loose on earth will be loosed in heaven."*

(Matt. 16:19, NIV)

## Basic Principles:

• God does not desire to withhold any good thing from you. The devil cannot keep any good thing from you, unless you let him. Only you can oppose your receiving all the spiritual blessings available in Christ Jesus.

• You can stop opposing your spiritual victory by binding yourself to the will and purposes of God and then stripping (loosing) away the old patterns and ways of your old nature, enlarging your capacity to receive renewal from Him.

• There are two main factors that will both affect and effect your Christian victory:
   1. Knowing how to stop opposing God's work in your life and
   2. knowing how to make room to receive from Him.

• Every believer comes to Christ with certain mind sets of misinformation. The mind is not instantly renewed at the moment of the Christian's new birth. Learn how to facilitate your own ability to receive renewal from Christ.

• God's work of renewal happens within the framework of where we are—in our minds, wills, and emotions that can be stuffed with past experiences and wrong beliefs protected by strongholds.

• A personal, inner stronghold is the **logic, reasoning, arguments, justifications, rationalizations, and denial you use to protect and defend your right to believe something—regardless of whether or not it is true.**

• Jesus has given us the keys to dealing with personal, inner strongholds—they are found in Matthew 16:19 and 18:18—binding and loosing principles.

• Binding an evil spirit to deactivate its power is only a temporary, front-line warfare strategy.

• Learn to seek for all facets of God's truth and then use His truth to gain freedom.

• Your fears and strongholds are the <u>only edge</u> Satan has ever had over you. You can loose them.

• Your real problem is not Satan, rather it is the vulnerability of your own damaged and broken soul and the strongholds it has erected for self-protection. This self-constructed protection effectively keeps the pain locked in, while keeping God's truth locked out. His truth is the only thing that will set you free.

• Strongholds not only permit Satan to have access to the unsurrendered, wounded soul, they also affect the believer's right standing with the Lord because they are built to justify and protect wrong attitudes, thoughts, and feelings.

• How do you know if you have any hidden inner strongholds? Ask yourself this question: **Is the will of God prospering in my life the way it should be, could be, and ought to be?** If you can answer yes, then you don't need this workbook. If your answer is no, then keep reading.

• Christianity is about <u>relationship and receiving</u>—relationship with and receiving from Jesus Christ. When your vertical relationship with Christ is fully realized, all of your horizontal relationships with others will be right. If you are filled with old fears and strongholds, you cannot enter into a fully free relationship with Christ because you don't have room within yourself to receive the strength and blessings that He wants to add to your positional standing of salvation in Him.

• Unfair, unkind, cruel things have happened to all of us—some more so than others. But, we are all responsible for the choices we make to hold on to their destructive, long-term effects.

• No higher level or broader scope of satanic strongholds will ever be effectively attacked and destroyed by those who are spiritually vulnerable because of their own personal, inner strongholds.

• You are not permanently bonded to the pain of your yesterdays. You can learn to loose wrong attitudes, wrong patterns of thinking, and the "self-layering" defense mechanisms that result from traumatic happenings, wrong misunderstandings, and mistakes in your past.

• If you desire a mate, learn to do a reality check on your motivations and desires for being married. Recognize the pitfalls of not waiting on God's healing for yourself. A strong, successful marriage in Christ grows out of bringing wholeness and strength to another person. Don't fall for the age-old deception that another person can finally make everything right in your life by fixing all of your unhealed hurts, unmet needs, and unresolved issues.

• Many turn away from wrong behaviors by sheer willpower, which takes a tremendous amount of mental, emotional, and physical energy to sustain. Learn how to get to the <u>internal sources of those behaviors</u> rather than depending solely on personal willpower to overcome their external manifestations.

• Learn to loose the power and effects of word curses spoken about you, to you, and by you.

• Realize that if you refuse to personally obey the same concepts in the Holy Scriptures that you are trying to confront Satan with, you will, effectively, give him legal ground in your life that he has every "right" to access.

• God will never forgive an unforgiving heart! Learn how to help an unforgiving heart to change.

• There is tremendous power in praying the binding and loosing prayers with others. This is the power of agreement.

• We don't own the Holy Spirit, can't contain the Holy Spirit, and we aren't called to orchestrate the workings of the Holy Spirit. The key to spiritual victory is knowing that all we are called to do is to surrender to Him!

• If you won't surrender your strongholds willingly, God will have to bring stress, frustration, and painful times to pressure you into coming out from behind them in order to be healed.

• You can pray for others and impact their lives whether or not they want God's help. Strongholds keep them from wanting help, and strongholds can be dealt with through loosing prayers!

• Binding and loosing prayers can shatter and destroy the effects of mistakes you made as a parent, including those now affecting your grandchildren as well.

• Binding and loosing prayers can have a tremendous impact on world leaders, government officials, and Israel.

• The world needs Christians right now. We need to tear down our strongholds, crush our wrong attitudes, smash our wrong beliefs, and destroy our wrong ideas so we are fully usable and available.

• In dealing with others, remember that those who oppose God, Christians, and themselves were not taught to make right choices. In fact, they were probably taught to make wrong choices.

• Bind yourself to the will of God and to the paths He wants you to walk so you can be used outside of your comfort zone. Learn to accept yourself and your value to others as God does.

• Only God knows how many strongholds you've built and how much fear is causing you to still oppose yourself and His work in you. But you can jump-start your own personal time schedule for victory.

• Every stone that falls from the strongholds you are loosing within yourself and within others allows a little space for Him to fill. And He will fill up every nook and cranny you create with His grace, mercy, power, healing, and love.

• Learn how to become very effective in changing lives, setting captives free, and redeeming precious time previously wasted in fighting the enemy.

# Group Study Guides

The following are some questions recommended for individual thought, as well as for group discussion in workshop sessions. Begin to think about how you feel about your answers. There are no right or wrong answers, rather the purpose of these questions is to jog your memory to bring hidden things to the surface and into the light of His love. In trying to answer these questions, even subtle emotional reactions can indicate areas where His love and light have not yet been able to enter and heal.

If you are pursuing this study on your own, write out your honest answers to these questions and pray over them. If you are unsure about your feelings and reactions to any questions in this workbook, feel free to write to Liberty Savard Ministries and we will agree in prayer with you, replying to your letter with encouragement and words of understanding.

1.   What specific things do you remember that your father taught you as a child?

2.   What do you remember your father doing or saying that gave you your first understanding of what love looked like, acted like, and sounded like?

3.   What specific things do you remember that your mother taught you as a child?

4.   What do you remember your mother doing or saying that gave you your first understanding of what love looked like, acted like, and sounded like?

5.   What do you remember that your father and/or mother told you about yourself and about your life?

> **These questions are asked in order to begin to bring buried feelings and wrong beliefs into your consciousness. We all tend to bring many things with us into our todays that are from our pasts. Unresolved memories, traumas, or misunderstandings from yesterday do affect our todays and our tomorrows. It is our prayer that you will, through the binding and loosing principles, be able to strip away much of your past's "baggage" and come to a place where you realize that your parents (grandparents, siblings, aunts, and uncles, etc.) did what they knew how to do as they raised you. Sad it may be, but they could not give you what they had not been given or taught themselves. Those imperfect people who have passed through our lives had imperfect people pass through the formative years of their lives. You can learn how to come out from behind the strongholds protecting the results of this generational pattern. You can also learn how not to become the imperfect person in other lives.**

6.   If you didn't know your birth parents, and if other adults such as grandparents, brothers, sisters, uncles, aunts, or adoptive parents played major roles in your early life, what are your remembrances of those adults?

7. What sticks out in your memory as the most profound things the adults of your life taught to you (positively or negatively) ?

8. What do you think your father thought of you?

9. What do you think your mother thought of you?

---

**A fair and honest anger at your parents and other authority figures of your past requires that you consider how they were trained to deal with their problems and needs—how much they were taught about unconditional love, receiving, and giving, etc. Should you then blame your grandparents? A fair and honest anger at your grandparents requires that you consider the same issues. Great-grandparents—same thing. The point is, how many generations do you want to go back to before you think you can finally place blame on the original perpetrator of the generational bondages that brought pain into your life?** *The key lies not in finding where to place the blame, but in releasing the protective layers you have placed over your own pain so that God can make you whole.*

**You can remove layers of self-defensive mechanisms you have placed over the unmet needs, unhealed hurts, and unresolved issues of your past. You do this by loosing (Matt. 16:19, Greek: smashing, crushing, destroying, tearing apart, and tearing down) the strongholds you have built around them. Only then can the healing grace and mercy of God flow freely into the wounded areas of vulnerability within your soul—your neediness, pain, and confusion.**

---

10. If you could have written a plan for your life from birth to now, what would you have wanted it to be like? Why?

11. If you could have it any way you wanted, what would you like the rest of your life to be like?

12. What do you think exists in your life at this time that could keep it from being like that?

13. What do you think is the biggest problem you face today?

14. If you could change anything about yourself, what would it be?

15. If you could change others in the family, who would you change the most and how?

16. As a child, what did you want to do when you grew up? Did you accomplish that goal? If your answer is no, what do you think kept you from succeeding?

---

**This workbook is designed to help you come to the realization that it is a fallacy to believe that if your parents (grandparents, siblings, aunts, uncles, spouse, children, etc.) would just stop saying things and doing things that hurt you and seem to hold you back, you would be all right. This is a self-defeating cycle that is based in the belief that further pain can only be avoided, and personal success can only be obtained by changing the behaviors of those around you.**

---

Effecting a cessation of hurtful behaviors from others will not meet your needs or resolve wounds deep within you. You need to break the cycles that evolve out of the belief that others could fix you if they would only . . . . (you fill in the blank).

God alone can and will make you whole, if you let Hin get to the unmet needs, unhealed hurts, and unresolved memories buried deep within your soul. Binding and loosing prayers strip away the layers you have laid down over these needs and hurts—binding and loosing prayers tear down the strongholds you have built to protect those layers and what they are covering. Then God can and will meet your needs and heal your hurts.

17. Describe God in your own words—not from Scriptures you know, but from your own perception of Him.

18. Can you find proof in the Word of God that your perception of Him and His feelings towards you are correct?

19. What are your personal beliefs of God today?

20. What do you think you should believe about God?

21. Do the answers to the last two questions agree?

22. How do you view prayer? As a petition of what you need? As a means of conversing with God? As an obligation that God will bless?

23. Do you feel that prayer works for you? How?

24. What caused you to come to Christ?

We all have had two pictures of God in our lives at one time or another. If you are very honest, you will probably find that you still do:

a) What you really think and feel about how God relates to you, and
b) What you know you are supposed to believe about God's love towards you based upon scriptural teaching and truth.

Binding and loosing prayers strip away wrong beliefs, wrong ideas, and wrong patterns of thinking that have kept you from being able to truly believe what you have been taught from the Bible and what you have read in the Bible.

25. What do you consider to be your strengths?

26. What do you consider to be your weaknesses?

27. What do you feel your greatest challenge in life is?

# General Instructions

1.  Record your specific prayers by date in the prayer journals provided at the end of every chapter in this study guide.

2.  Faithfully use the binding and loosing "keys to effective prayer" to affect their answers.

3.  Use the log at the end of each workbook chapter to record the answers to your prayers.

4.  Pay close attention to word curses that you may have previously spoken or you may be speaking about yourself and about others. Loose the word curses spoken about you, to you, and by you. What is a word curse? Any words that are unkind, unloving, uncomplimentary, unforgiving, unsupportive, manipulative, controlling, hard, harsh, critical, cruel, judgmental, sarcastic, or condemning—any words that do not bring blessing.

5.  Begin to recognize the word curses that others—parents, family members, friends, teachers, etc.—have said about you or to you as a child, or may be saying to you now. Begin to concentrate, not on the words spoken to you, but on loosing (from your life) the effects of those word curses. At the same time, concentrate on also loosing wrong reactions and thought patterns from yourself that negative words set into motion in your unsurrendered soul. Determine that you will not perpetuate the word curses with your own mouth, "... *for out of the abundance of the heart, the mouth speaketh"* (Matt. 12:34, see also Luke 6:45). Record what you have learned about yourself each week.

6.  Concentrate on loosing all strongholds associated with and protecting the sources of fear in your life. Record the fears you find yourself dealing with. Record what the loosing of them brings about in your life.

7.  Keep referring to the following Scriptures and any others you can find in your Bible regarding fear:

> *"There is no fear in love; but perfect love casteth out fear: because fear hath torment. He that feareth is not made perfect in love."* (1 John 4:18, KJV)

> *"We need have no fear of someone who loves us perfectly; his perfect love for us eliminates all dread of what he might do to us. If we are afraid, it is for fear of what he might do to us, and shows that we are not fully convinced that he really loves us."* (1 John 4:18, TLB)

> *"Love has no fear in it; instead, perfect love expels fear, for fear involves punishment. Therefore he who fears has not reached love's perfection."* (1 John 4:18, Modern Language Version)

*"There is no fear in love—dread does not exist; but full-grown (complete, perfect) love turns fear out of doors and expels every trace of terror! For fear brings with it the thought of punishment and (so) he who is afraid has not reached the full maturity of love—is not yet grown into love's complete perfection."* (1 John 4:18, TAB)

8.  Why are you participating in group discussion sessions (or completing the workbook on your own) of *Shattering Your Strongholds*?

9.  What results do you expect from using the binding and loosing principles?

10. Write each of the following Scriptures out in your favorite translation. Try to commit them to memory.

Titus 3:5

_____

_____

_____

_____

Philippians 2:13

_____

_____

_____

_____

Jeremiah 29:11

_____

_____

_____

_____

Matthew 16:19

_____

_____

_____

_____

Hebrews 5:13,14

_____

_____

_____

_____

Galatians 3:28-29

_____
_____
_____
_____

11. Begin now to keep a personal journal of your journey in *Shattering Your Strongholds* (journal space after each lesson). We have a tendency to forget many things God does for us unless we write them down. Because of that, we suggest you use this workbook to chronicle your journey with *Shattering Your Strongholds*. It will serve to encourage you during the seemingly "quiet" times of your growth when you feel like nothing is happening.

> **It is important to remember that even though you don't "see" anything happening in the natural realm, God is moving mountains in the spiritual realm for you because you have chosen to align your will with His! Pray for the manifestation in the natural realm of what is being accomplished in the spiritual realm by the power of His Spirit.**

12. Be faithful in recording entries in your prayer journal for great encouragement during those "quiet" times. God often admonished His people in the Old Testament to make memorials and to have special times of remembrances. You need to do this, too.

# Individual and Group Discussion Syllabus

## Purposes:

• To help you <u>develop and exercise</u> the binding and loosing "tools" you have learned to use by reading *Shattering Your Strongholds*.

• To give you encouragement until you are able to handle any challenge that the shattering of your own strongholds may present to you.

• To guide you through an understanding of what happens when the strongholds come down in your life so <u>you do not react to</u>, but rather, <u>you do cooperate with</u> what God is doing.

• To steady you when long-buried hurts and unmet needs are finally exposed, so you can allow His healing to flow freely into them.

• To show you how to hold on when there seems to be no outward expression of change, and to hold on even stronger when the change does come.

• To teach you how to not oppose your own healing and deliverance.

## Expected Results:

• That you will experience great growth in your personal life as your unsurrendered soul begins to lose its control over your actions and reactions.

• That you will learn to cooperate with what God is working out in your life so that you will become strong and dangerous to the enemy.

• That every person completing the workbook, whether individually or in a discussion group, will become strong enough to help others experience major breakthroughs as well.

• That you will become part of a core of prayer warriors in the body of Christ who are willing to pray for others embarking on this same journey.

• That you will use the keys of the Kingdom to pray them on through to victory!

• That the body of Christ will grow strong and be able to positively impact the lives of many others for Christ.

## Basic Guidelines to Follow in a Discussion Group:

1. Nothing discussed about any private situations, feelings, needs, etc., must ever leave the group setting. Total confidentiality is important.

2. Everyone is to respect each others thoughts and feelings at all times.

3. A solid commitment to regular attendance and daily use of binding and loosing prayers is expected.

4. There can be <u>no other</u> involvement in any other self-help groups or philosophies for the ten-week duration of the discussion group.

5. While in the group, the principles of praying will be according to the principles of the binding and loosing concepts taken from *Shattering Your Strongholds*.

## What a *Shattering Your Strongholds* Discussion Group <u>IS NOT:</u>

A *Shattering Your Strongholds* discussion group is not a therapy group, nor a social group. You are not to come together to psychoanalyze each other or to counsel each other. Nor should you consider the group a social night for fellowshipping with others.

## What a *Shattering Your Strongholds* Discussion Group <u>IS:</u>

The group leader should have definitely studied the book *Shattering Your Strongholds*. He or she should also be somewhat <u>experienced in and currently using the binding and loosing prayers.</u> The leader should be binding his or her own mind to the mind of Christ, praying for direction and understanding for the group. Group leaders are welcome to contact Liberty Savard Ministries by mail, e-mail, or fax (see ministry address, e-mail, and fax number in back of book) for questions they are unable to answer, or for encouragement and/or guidance for starting or implementing a *Shattering Your Strongholds* discussion group.

When the leader asks how your week was, he or she is attempting to define how you are doing with your spiritual "tools" of binding and loosing. Have you been using them in a productive manner? Have they assisted you in tearing down strongholds? Have they helped you overcome situations that could have previously caused you to stumble or fall? Did you have any breakthroughs because of your new prayers of binding and loosing? Are you having any specific problems or questions you would like to have clarified?

The purpose of the workbook/discussion group is to guide you in your use of the binding and loosing prayers; to give you road signs and to point out what is happening in your life. Also, to give you guidance about how you can align yourself with the Holy Spirit of God as He shows you areas of strongholds that you have previously been avoiding or have been unaware of in your life.

It is the leader's job to get you back on track if you are beginning to move away from focusing in on a stronghold. Due to time limitations and the number of participants in a given group, there are times when he or she must prevent excessive, unnecessary explanations of details unless they are truly relevant. Each person in a group should be allowed to participate (asking questions, relating prayer experiences, clarifying points, etc.) during every session. While everyone should feel free to share, all should be aware of everyone else's need for expression and asking questions. Groups are usually most functional when kept between eight to fifteen members.

When someone else is sharing, please do not try to interject your own thoughts and feelings about someone else's story unless the leader opens the floor for group input. Often, in an attempt to "identify" with and help someone, you may accidentally break the flow of the Holy Spirit's dealings with an individual and the moment is lost. The Lord may have to walk that person through the same painful dealings they have already experienced during the previous week in order to bring them back to a point of being able to disclose a hidden fear or buried need.

It is crucial that you remain in a prayerful, listening attitude of respect when others are speaking—and especially when they have finished and the leader is responding to them. The leader will have prepared himself or herself through study of the Word and prayer to be used by the Holy Spirit to receive insight and words of guidance from God's Spirit. He or she needs to hear the quiet voice of the Spirit at that critical time. If you feel the Holy Spirit has spoken a word to you regarding the persons circumstances, please be very sensitive to the Holy Spirit and the leader so as to know when to share that word.

## What Can You Expect Individually, or in a Group Setting?

Each person using this workbook will be in a different stage of growth and at different levels of awareness concerning his or her needs, hurts, and unresolved issues. However, the truths you have learned from *Shattering Your Strongholds* will work in whatever stage you find yourself. The binding and loosing keys of the Kingdom are valid regardless of how aware of your strongholds you are. It is not necessary, practical, nor even possible, that you identify, name, and specifically focus on every stronghold in your life.

One of the best aspects of using this scriptural principle is that you can work on your strongholds "in general" and see many walls begin to come down. The Lord will lead you into recognizing specific strongholds if necessary. When He does, the understanding of them will come easily. Do not get bogged down and tangled up in trying to name and identify specific areas He has not yet revealed.

You will learn how to strip off the layers covering the areas of vulnerability that God wants to heal. You will come to understand unmet needs in your life and how they have manifested themselves in ways you've never realized. You will learn to look at and deal with the undesired levels of impact on your life that others are having, even to the point of keeping you in bondage.

### YOU WILL LEARN HOW TO CONQUER YOUR FEARS
### AND SHATTER YOUR STRONGHOLDS!

# Foreword

## (from *Shattering Your Strongholds*)

1.  What makes us worthy to receive from God?

    _____

    _____

    _____

    _____

2.  If you do not experience spiritual wisdom, power, understanding, answers, and peace, who do you blame?  Who should you blame?  Who shouldn't you blame?

    _____

    _____

    _____

    _____

3.  Do you think God would withhold these good things from you?  If so, why?

    _____

    _____

4.  Can the devil keep these things from you?  If so, how?

    _____

    _____

5.  Do you have to "earn" God's blessings to receive from Him?  If so, how can you personally earn them?

    _____

    _____

    _____

    _____

6. Do you think the quantity of prayer and Bible reading you do increases God's willingness to bless you?  Why?

_____

_____

7. What must you do to enlarge your capacity to receive from God?

_____

_____

8. Do you think you have opposed God's work in your life?  Explain your response, whether yes or no.

_____

_____

# 1
# The Keys to the Kingdom

1. What is the bottom-line, basic truth all Christians need to know?

_____

_____

2. Is this "basic" truth all you need in order to live an overcoming life while here on earth?

_____

_____

3. What are the two different sides of seeking for inner truth? What occurs to cause too many Christians to quit seeking truth?

_____

_____

_____

_____

4. How would you describe one-dimensional understanding and its requirement and cost?

_____

_____

_____

_____

5. What happens when we are always seeking truth?

_____

_____

_____

_____

6. Baby Christians (immature Christians) cannot do what? They only know how to do what? With what do you generally nourish such a baby Christian?

_____

_____

_____

_____

7.  The spiritually mature Christian cannot survive on what kind of diet?

_____
_____

8.  Hebrews 5:13-14 (NIV) tells us what kind of food is for the mature Christian and how this Christian trains himself or herself. Explain your understanding of these verses.

_____
_____
_____
_____
_____

9.  Spoiled meat can kill you. How does this analogy relate to the meat of the Scriptures?

_____
_____
_____
_____

10. In what manner should we handle the Word of God?

_____
_____
_____
_____

## Old Mind Sets

11. What does every believer come to Christ with? If these things are deeply entrenched and resistant to renewal, what can the believer come dangerously close to?

_____
_____
_____

12. You can actually have two different pictures of God. What are they?

_____
_____
_____

13. What you learn about God comes to you through what filters? What are some of your ideas about God that you have had to struggle to change?

_____
_____
_____
_____

14. What do many in church leadership assume that scriptural teaching will automatically do?

_____

_____

_____

_____

15. What is the problem with this assumption?

_____

_____

16. Within what framework does God's work of renewal occur? Rather than changing, bypassing, or overriding your will, what will God do?

_____

_____

_____

_____

17. What can distort the spiritual truth you read from God's Word?

_____

_____

18. Is the Christian's mind automatically renewed at his or her new birth?

_____

_____

19. What process do we have to use to effect this renewal?

_____

_____

## Self-Erected Strongholds

20. How do our minds come into salvation?

_____

_____

21. What is the key to receiving renewal as fast as possible?

_____

_____

22. When this renewal is not received, what do some Christians spend their lives doing?

_____

_____

_____

_____

23. What do many Christians mistakenly use as a guideline for forming their concept of God?

_____

_____

24. What causes us to believe that when we fail, God turns His back on us?

_____

_____

25. Jesus gave us keys to tear down wrong ideas, flawed concepts, doubts, and distortions. What are they? What is the enemy attempting to destroy in your life?

_____

_____

_____

_____

26. Why are you and I here?

_____

_____

27. How do many in the Church today see themselves?

_____

_____

28. How can you have an impact on someone else's life without their permission?

_____

_____

## The New Creature Process

29. Being a new creature in Christ results from what factors? A new creature with old things passed away has the right to what?

_____

_____

_____

_____

30. As a new, born-again believer, what happens that can make you feel totally undone?

_____

_____

31. With regard to Titus 3:5 (NIV), many have experienced the rebirth referenced, but what may they still hold on to? Why?

_____

_____

32. What has to happen in order to bring your life on earth into alignment with God's will in heaven?

_____

_____

33. Does God play any part in this choice? (See Phil. 2:13, TAB.) If so, what part does He play?

_____

_____

_____

_____

## A Hope and A Future

34. Are you a believer who fully trusts and expects the promises of God's Word to be manifested in your own life, or do you struggle with accepting Scriptures such as Jeremiah 29:11?

_____

_____

_____

_____

35. What is the general "personality profile" of those who do resist Jeremiah 29:11? Does this sound familiar to any part of your "personality profile"?

_____

_____

_____

_____

36. Saying that the principles in *Shattering Your Strongholds* are not intended to conflict with any other prayer and spiritual warfare concepts, who and what does the author then liken the understanding to?

_____

_____

_____

_____

37. What does "heaven" mean in Matthew 16:19? Matthew 18:18?

_____

_____

38. Write out Matthew 16:19 from your favorite translation:

_____

_____

_____

_____

39. In order to transact spiritual business, Christ gave us keys.  What three things do those keys represent to us?

_____

_____

40. What does the binding and loosing described in Matthew 16:19 represent to us?

_____

_____

41. What are the original Greek words for "bind," and what do they mean?  Write out all the meanings.

_____

_____

_____

_____

42. What is the Greek word for "loose," and the two words mentioned in the text as root words closely associated with the word "loose"?  Write out their complete meanings.

_____

_____

_____

_____

_____

_____

_____

43. What are you really saying when you loose a person from a bondage?  (Use the "splinter principle" to remember whether to loose a person or the problem:  You don't loose or take the person away from a splinter in their flesh, you loose or take away the splinter.)

_____

_____

_____

_____

44. Do you think you have not searched for the whole truth?  If so, why not?

_____

_____

_____

_____

# Chapter 1 - Review

**The most significant truths I found in this chapter are:**

1. _____
_____
_____

2. _____
_____
_____

3. _____
_____
_____

4. _____
_____
_____

**I applied these truths to my life as follows:**

1. _____
_____
_____

2. _____
_____
_____

3. _____
_____
_____

4. _____
_____
_____

# Chapter 1 - "Journey" Journal

**Date:**                    **Questions I have:**

**Date:**                    **Special insights I believe I have learned:**

**Date:**                    **Breakthroughs I have experienced:**

# Chapter 1 - Prayer Journal

**Date:**                   **Prayer:**

**Date:**                   **Updates and special encouragements I've received from the Lord:**

**Date:**                   **Answers to prayers:**

# 2
# The Rest of the Truth

**Puzzle Pieces**

| God won't use you very much if you don't have foundation balance. He doesn't want you to fall over! |
| --- |

1.  There is a purpose and an order to the arranging of the "pieces" in our lives.  Explain your understanding of the example of the "puzzle pieces."

_____
_____
_____
_____

Can you relate this example to any given time of your life?

_____
_____
_____
_____

2.  What further complicates how  the puzzle pieces of our lives will finally look when they are all fit together?

_____
_____
_____
_____

3.  What does the Holy Spirit's placing of the border pieces in your "puzzle" reflect?

_____
_____
_____
_____

4. Why is it true that so many of the prettiest, biggest, and brightest puzzle pieces we want to run with won't fit anywhere in our lives when we want them to?

_____

_____

5. Name some of the foundational pieces that must be in place in our lives before God can really use us:

_____

_____

_____

_____

6. How careful are you to faithfully search in the Word of God to see if what you are being taught is the truth?

_____

_____

7. What do we tend to do as a result of concentrating so intensely on single facets of information that we've been taught?

_____

_____

8. Spiritual food that is tasty, easy-to-chew, and delivered quickly is still the diet of choice for many Christians. From one who learned the hard way, "Such a spiritual diet will

_____   _____   _____ when your back is to the wall and Satan is reaching for everything you have."

Has your back ever been to the wall? When?

_____

_____

_____

_____

How did you deal with that situation?

_____

_____

_____

_____

Having the truth you now possess, what would you have done differently?

_____

_____

_____

_____

9. We need spiritual truth that <u>we know that we know</u>. What kind of truth is this?

_____

_____

10. John 8:31-32 says:

_____

_____

_____

_____

11.  When do we profit most from what someone else has learned?

_____

_____

_____

_____

12. You can have all _____ and still be _____ if you have not tried to do anything _____ _____ .

13. In the original Greek text, one of the meanings for truth is: _____
_____ _____ .

14. You have to _____ and _____ _____ truth to see what yet may be _____ from your _____ of it.

15. Wisdom comes from _____ _____ and then
_____ _____ and _____ .

16. Ephesians 3:19 (TAB) says:

_____

_____

_____

17. When someone else opens up a new understanding for you, in what form does it remain if you don't act upon it?

_____

_____

_____

_____

18. Second-hand _____ is generally accompanied by second-hand

_____ .

19. How do most Christians learn about praying, warfare, witnessing, and interacting with other believers?

_____

_____

_____

_____

Is this an acceptable way of learning the first steps of the Christian walk?

_____

_____

20. You will only learn about relationship with Christ and His truth by what?

_____

_____

_____

_____

## Discover Your Special Plan and Purpose

> **Our God is a very personal God.**
> **He loves you intensely, having made you with a unique potential**
> **to bring joy and pleasure to Him in a way no other human being can .**
> **You are incredibly special to Him.**

21. What stone can God's truth be compared to?  Explain your understanding of this comparison.

_____

_____

_____

_____

22. The acceptance of truth in its simplest form often leaves much to be learned.  When does this usually seem to happen?

_____

_____

_____

_____

23. "Reading the Bible diligently is not enough."  Please give your understanding of this statement as explained in the text of the book.

_____

_____

Is one-dimensional understanding all there is for some of us?  Explain your answer.

_____

_____

24. What must we do with truth in order to receive freedom?

_____

_____

_____

_____

25. Regarding the story of the little child's living conditions, did any of the additional truths make the child's original statement of truth incorrect, or did they enhance your understanding of the original answer the child gave?

_____

_____

If you had not known the latter facets of the truth, what would your understanding be?

_____

_____

_____

_____

26. What happens when we accept someone else's understanding as our own personal truth?

_____

_____

27. Does reading the Bible guarantee spiritual wisdom and understanding? Explain your answer.

_____

_____

_____

_____

28. John 5:39-40 (TAB) says:

_____

_____

_____

_____

_____

_____

Circle what you consider to be the <u>key words</u> of the above Scriptures.

29. What were the religious Jews of Jesus' time missing in their lives?

_____

_____

## Experiencing the Word of God

30. What is your understanding of the bicycle word-picture in this section and how can you relate to it?

_____

_____

_____

_____

_____

31. What must you do in order for textbook teachings to be more than collections of words?

_____

_____

_____

_____

32. Many life-giving concepts in the Word become _____,

_____, _____ you will never forget when those concepts

become _____ in your life.

33. Faith does indeed come by _____ _____ _____,

but faith grows by _____ the Word.

34. Faith and experience turn _____ into _____

_____ .

> **We relate to the world around us in our human mortal state differently
> from the way we relate to God's truth in our spirits.**

35. You have communion with God _____ your _____ .

36. Your body is in touch with the earthly things of the world around you,

_____ and _____ through the senses of _____,

_____, _____, _____ and _____ .

37. Your soul can be loosely likened to your _____, consisting of your

_____, _____ and _____ .

38. Your _____, _____ and your _____ make

up who _____ are—a fearfully and _____ made

_____ _____ .

39. Explain in your own words what similarities our mind has to a computer.

_____

_____

_____

_____

_____

40. Explain your understanding of the comparison between your emotions and spices.

_____

_____

_____

_____

41. Fight, flight, fidget, or file for later.  Sometimes your will authorizes a _____,
quite the _____ of what your _____ would advise.

42. The example of the conference room shows an unwise response based on inaccurate
perceptions.  Have you experienced a situation where you completely misunderstood what
was actually happening, and reacted unwisely based on your tarnished perceptions?  Give an
example.

_____
_____
_____
_____

43. What must be submitted to the will of God in order for you to respond wisely to your
circumstances?

a) _____          b) _____          c) _____ .

44. If you are not surrendered to God's will and the truth, what will you generally listen to?
What do you suppose the outcome of most of those decisions will be?

_____
_____
_____
_____

45. What is the key to spiritual success?

_____
_____

46. What was the best choice you ever made?

_____
_____
_____
_____

47. What does Romans 8:28 say about the wrong choices we may make?

_____
_____
_____
_____

48. Can we start over with God?  What extra baggage will He make us carry?

_____
_____

49. What places our past under the blood of Jesus?

_____
_____

50. Is God's plan and purpose for you limited and diminished because you messed up in the past? Explain your answer.

_____

_____

51. Your _____, your _____, your _____ with the Lord and others will only be _____ by your inability to receive God's _____ .

52. You are only limited by the _____ you _____ from this minute forward.


## Know Your Enemy

53. What is the only edge Satan has ever had in your life since you became a Christian?

Your _____ and _____ .

54. How has he been using them?

_____

_____

_____

_____

55. What erroneous belief has caused you cooperate with his attacks on you?

_____

_____

56. What does the Greek word *ochuroma* mean? _____ .

57. What is the full definition of an *ochuroma?*

_____

_____

_____

_____

_____

_____

58. If we have believed a lie about ourselves, we will fight to protect that belief. What do we end up doing by this process?

_____

_____

59. What often happens when others attempt to convince you that you are believing a lie?

_____

_____

60. Can our unmet needs be used against us?  If yes, then how?

_____
_____
_____
_____
_____
_____

61. Is Satan the root of your problem?  Explain your answer.

_____
_____

## The Root Problem

62. The root problem of our lack of victory and overcoming is the _____ of a _____ _____ and its _____ .

63. Erected by a _____ _____ to keep further _____ out, these _____ keep the _____ in.

64. Erected by a _____ _____ to protect _____ which were birthed from _____ _____ , these _____ keep _____ _____ out. _____ knows exactly what kind of _____ you will erect to protect your _____ _____ , _____ , _____ and _____ _____ . He _____ _____ to access these and batter your _____ further, impacting your _____ _____ .

65. We have all been used and abused in the past.  Is that our problem now? _____ .

66. Having been used and abused, what should our next decision be?

_____
_____
_____
_____

67. Using your Bible, find and write down the chapter and verse where God's Word says that "He that is in you is greater than he that is in the world." Based on that Scripture, is Satan your problem?

_____
_____
_____
_____

68. Are God's love, promises, and faithfulness toward the believer unchangeable? What does this tell us?

_____

_____

_____

_____

69. What is the believer's problem?

_____

_____

_____

_____

70. What makes it possible to crucify the old nature?  What will you receive when you do it?

_____

_____

_____

_____

71. Do you have to throw away the truth you have in order to receive new truth? Why?

_____

_____

_____

_____

# Chapter 2 - Review

**The most significant truths I found in this chapter are:**

1. _____
_____
_____

2. _____
_____
_____

3. _____
_____
_____

4. _____
_____
_____

**I applied these truths to my life as follows:**

1. _____
_____
_____

2. _____
_____
_____

3. _____
_____
_____

4. _____
_____
_____

# Chapter 2 - "Journey" Journal

**Date:**                    **Questions I have:**

**Date:**                    **Special insights I believe I have learned:**

**Date:**                    **Breakthroughs I have experienced:**

# Chapter 2 - Prayer Journal

**Date:**                    **Prayer:**

**Date:**                    **Updates and special encouragements I've received from the Lord:**

**Date:**                    **Answers to prayers:**

# 3
# A New Look at Old Things

## New Creatures or Spiritual Accidents?

1. In your own words, what do the following words mean to you?

Love:

_____

_____

Trust:

_____

_____

Mercy:

_____

_____

2. What was Trudy's main problem with receiving truth?

_____

_____

3. The author says that every time other Christians tried to share the truth with Trudy, she experienced "emotional whiplash." What do you think this means?

_____

_____

4. What was twisting the pure truth from the Word of God that was offered again and again to Trudy over the years?

_____

_____

5.  Is your past more powerful in your life than the Word of God?

_____

_____

## Clogged Filters

6.  Our minds have been used to functioning as what?

_____

_____

7.  A mind filled with _____ _____ and _____ _____ from the past is a mind clogged with _____, and it will _____ and _____ the _____ it receives today.

8.  What becomes the source of the strongholds protecting distorted ideas, attitudes, and patterns of thinking today?

_____

_____

_____

_____

9.  God's love, mercy, and faithfulness eventually broke through Trudy's mistrust and fear, but what was lost during this process that she constantly opposed?

_____

_____

_____

_____

10. What did Satan use to make Trudy build her walls of distrust and fear?

_____

_____

_____

_____

11. What did Trudy program herself to receive?  What did that allow Satan to do?

_____

_____

_____

_____

12. God will use time to make our faith grow, but all too often delays in our lives are what?

_____

_____

13. Isaiah 55:8-9 says:

_____
_____
_____
_____

## Doors of Access

14. What is your understanding of what the author calls "doors of access"?

_____
_____
_____
_____

15. James 4:7 (NIV) says:

_____
_____

16. Will God condone strongholds in your life if you've been hurt very, very deeply?

_____
_____

17. What will God not allow you to hold onto and still be able to enter into the fullness of your inheritance?

_____
_____

## Right Standing With God

18. What are the translations of the Greek word for "evil" in 1 Peter 3:12 (TAB)?

_____
_____
_____
_____

19. Strongholds affect the believer's right standing with the Lord by protecting _____  _____, _____ and feelings.

20. God is attentive to the prayers of those who:

_____
_____

His face is against those who:

_____

_____

21. Can you cause God to oppose, frustrate, and defeat you in your prayers?  If yes, how?

_____

_____

22. James 5:16 says:

_____

_____

23. Job 22:30 (TAB) says:

_____

_____

_____

_____

24. Job 42:7-8 (NIV) says:

_____

_____

_____

_____

25. When and/or how is a stronghold reinforced?

_____

_____

_____

_____

26. What are the three examples listed of how believers may feel about their strongholds?

a) _____

_____

b) _____

_____

c) _____

_____

27. Why do you think some Christians equate facing reality with disbelief and doubt?

_____

_____

28. There are times when you have to be _____ _____ to _____ what is keeping you from _____ God's plan for your life.

## Reconciliation and Restoration Promised

29. 2 Corinthians 5:18-19 says:

_____

_____

_____

_____

What is the Greek word for reconciliation?  What does it mean in addition to reconciliation?

_____

_____

_____

_____

30.  Romans 12:2 says:

_____

_____

_____

_____

31. The word "renew" means to:

_____

_____

32. What has to happen before a restoration project can begin on an old house?

_____

_____

33. How can the examples of the prophet's widow and Elisha and Jesus and the wedding related on page 41 of the book be applied to your life?

_____

_____

_____

_____

34. The Amplified Bible states in Acts 3:19-21, "*So repent—change your mind and purpose; turn around and return (to God), that your sins may be erased (blotted out, wiped clean), that times of _____ —of _____ from the effects of heat, of _____ with fresh air—may come from the presence of the Lord; and He may send (to you) the Christ, the Messiah, Who before was _____ and _____ for you, Jesus, whom heaven must receive (and retain) until the time for the _____ _____ of all that God spoke by the _____ of all the prophets for ages past—from the most ancient times in the memory of man.*"

35. There are four Scriptures on pages 42 and 43.  List their references and a key word (your choice) in each Scripture.

_____

_____

_____

_____

36. What will the Prophet Elijah do before the great and terrible day of the Lord?

_____

_____

_____

_____

37. Where has God said He will put His law in our day?

_____

_____

38. What does God say He will restore to us?

_____

_____

_____

_____

39. How are we transformed?

_____

_____

## Receiving Restoration and Renewal

40. Why are so many Christians not receiving and experiencing restoration and renewal or power in these last days?

_____

_____

41. Who can walk in the Spirit and do what Jesus did in these last days?

_____

_____

42. What is the proof of your freedom from the effects of your past experiences?

_____

_____

43. When is hell able to sustain its program against you ?

_____

_____

44. If you are like a house opposing itself, how does this affect your resistance to the enemy?

_____
_____
_____
_____

45. Those who are supposed to have the answers are generally in what shape themselves?

_____
_____
_____
_____

## Struggling Cannot Bring Renewal

46. Name two of the problems (listed in the text) with the theory that wounded people need to directly confront the one who wounded them. Can you think of any other problems with this supposed method of attaining a healing?

_____
_____
_____
_____

47. What does the author say "enables us to avoid dealing directly with God"? Have you seen this in your own life?

_____
_____
_____
_____

48. With regard to twelve-step programs, the author lists one potentially positive outcome and one potentially negative outcome of these groups. What are they?

_____
_____
_____
_____
_____
_____

> **It is recommended that you do not participate in any twelve-step programs or self-help groups while taking the *Shattering Your Strongholds* workshops. The reason for this is: Through the use of the binding and loosing prayers, you may be led to a point where you are about to break through a stronghold, <u>but it doesn't quite happen</u>. Participating in another group frequently will cause you to recycle old patterns and either re-bury or "own" the source (the strongholds is protecting) all over again.**

49. The Bible personalities mentioned on page 47 are good examples of those who dealt directly with God for their problems:

Saul of Tarsus, for his _____

Peter, for his _____

Moses, for his _____

David, for _____

Woman _____

---

**Basically what Jesus was saying to the woman in John 8:11 was <u>that there were none who had the courage to stand in His presence and accuse her of anything.</u>** Jesus says the same thing to us today:
**There is no condemnation to those who are in Him (Romans 8:1).**

---

50. Can you heal yourself by a strong will to survive?

_____

_____

51. If a counselor, program, or group helps you come to the point of realizing you have to deal directly with God for your healing, they have served you well—but they cannot do what?

_____

_____

52. The only way to be truly free is to _____ your old _____ of everything it _____ _____ from, _____ down the _____ you have _____ and then allow _____ to spiritually _____ your _____ .

## Understanding Strongholds

53. What was one possibly "positive" use of strongholds in a life that explains why someone trusts them in the first place?

_____

_____

_____

_____

54. If strongholds are still in place in your life, what are they providing?

_____

_____

55. What have you often learned to trust more than you trust the truth?

_____

_____

56. Once more: What is a stronghold?

_____

_____

_____

_____

57. Here is a list of a few of the areas where we build strongholds. How do each of these areas cause us to behave?

Suspicion:

_____

_____

Doubt:

_____

_____

Independence:

_____

_____

False Security:

_____

_____

Confusion:

_____

_____

Unforgiveness:

_____

_____

Distrust:

_____

_____

Control and Manipulation:

_____

_____

Self-indulgence:

_____

_____

Fear:

_____

_____

Denial:

_____

_____

58. We have to _____ to make room to receive the renewal and restoration that will replace old things in our lives.

59. God generally will _____ _____ _____ what you don't want to surrender.

60. Will Jesus make us accept His help if we're desperate enough? _____.

61. When are we the strongest?

_____

_____

62. What can be more powerful in shaping your life than the truth?

_____

_____

63. You need God's help in what way after you have begun to sort through the bits and pieces of truth that you have?

_____

_____

# Chapter 3 - Review

**The most significant truths I found in this chapter are:**

1. _____
_____
_____

2. _____
_____
_____

3. _____
_____
_____

4. _____
_____
_____

**I applied these truths to my life as follows:**

1. _____
_____
_____

2. _____
_____
_____

3. _____
_____
_____

4. _____
_____
_____

# Chapter 3 - "Journey" Journal

**Date:**                    **Questions I have:**

**Date:**                    **Special insights I believe I have learned:**

**Date:**                    **Breakthroughs I have experienced:**

# Chapter 3 - Prayer Journal

**Date:**                    **Prayer:**

**Date:**                    **Updates and special encouragements I've received from the Lord:**

**Date:**                    **Answers to prayers:**

# 4
# Binding

## Two Kinds of Binding

1.  What are the two sides of binding?

_____

_____

2.  What does the Hebrew word *qashar* (from the Old Testament) mean?

_____

_____

3.  Referring to the value of God's wisdom and truth, the author references three Scriptures. What are they? Choose a key word in each.

a) _____
b) _____
c) _____

4.  What are the three areas to which these Scriptures say we are to bind mercy and truth?

a) _____
b) _____
c) _____

5.  How does Isaiah 61:1 (KJV) use two different sides of the words expressing binding or bound?

_____

_____

_____

_____

6.  What does the Hebrew word *chabash* (used for bind) mean?

_____

_____

7.  What does the Hebrew word *acar* (used for bound) mean?

_____

_____

8.  What is your understanding of the examples of the baby wrap used by the author?

_____

_____

_____

_____

9.  Why does it make sense to bind yourself to the steadfast things of God?

_____

_____

_____

_____

10. As the author began to bind herself to the things of God, what happened in her inner man?

_____

_____

11. With Matthew 6:9-10, 16:19 and 18:18 in mind, what does binding your will to God's will do?

_____

_____

_____

_____

12. Is the statement "deception always comes at the child of God in pure black" true or false?

13. What second step is prudent when you bind yourself to the truth of God?

_____

_____

_____

_____

14. When we bind ourselves to the truth we begin to see people and situations differently. What do we often begin to see?  How will that change our reactions to others?

_____

_____

_____

_____

15. To what is it good to bind ourselves and why?

_____

_____

_____

_____

16. What are the benefits of binding yourself to an awareness of the blood of Jesus?

_____

_____

_____

_____

## A Strengthened and Steadied Mind

17. What can happen when you allow your mind to dwell on situations in your past, perhaps even rewriting their outcome according to what you wish you had said or done?

_____

_____

_____

_____

18. The author references three Scriptures in regard to the mind. What are they?

a) _____

b) _____

c) _____

19. What combination of binding prayers would cause old patterns of thinking to back off?

_____

_____

20. Another word for bind, *sumbiazo* (Greek), is used in Ephesians 4:16. What does that Scripture say?

_____

_____

_____

_____

21. *Thayer's Greek-English Lexicon* describes "compacted" (as used in Eph. 4:16) as:

_____

_____

_____

_____

22. What is a powerful key you can use in situations where you do not know how to meet the hidden or revealed expectations of others?

_____

_____

_____

_____

## 911 Emergency

23. Psalm 91:1 (TAB) says:

_____

_____

_____

_____

_____

_____

## Partaking

24. There are three scriptural references listed for "partaking." What are they and what does each one say we can partake of?

a) _____

b) _____

c). _____

25. The Greek word translated as partaker means _____, _____,

_____, _____ .

26. "As I bind myself to the truth and to God's will for my life, I am a participant in the

_____ _____, which has always been the _____

of the _____ . My will comes together and begins to _____

with His will."

27. The writer expresses her feelings as she binds her mind to Christ's mind. What are those responses? How do you respond when your mind is bound to the mind of Christ?

_____

_____

_____

_____

28. How often do you use your "keys" during a day? Do you remember to use them when you face things that make you feel undone? If your answer is no, how do you think you can change that?

_____

_____

_____

_____

_____

_____

29. The writer expresses her feelings as she binds herself to the blood of Jesus and the work of the Cross. What does she do and what is she aware of? What do you experience when you use these forms of binding?

_____
_____
_____
_____

## Dealing With Evil Spirits

30. Did Jesus and His disciples name and bind the evil spirits when they spoke to them? What did they do?

_____
_____
_____
_____

31. There are three "types" of spirits we have to deal with—name them:

a) _____
b) _____
c) _____

32. What are angels sent to do for us?

_____
_____
_____
_____

33. What can cause believers to deny their own culpability in a situation?

_____
_____
_____
_____

34. When we blame all negative situations on evil spirits, what does this enable us to avoid addressing?

_____
_____
_____
_____

35. When we see our personal goals and desires being thwarted, what is the risk we run in automatically blaming Satan?

_____
_____

36. What is stated as the basic flaw in the act of binding (the imprisoning side of binding) evil spirits?

_____

_____

37. Strongholds create the _____ _____ in the human _____ that _____ _____ can _____.

38. You can bind the "spirit" of lying (hate, infirmity, etc.) innumerable times and the person can remain in the same kind of bondage. If "whatsoever" you bind on earth is bound in heaven, how can this happen?

_____

_____

_____

_____

39. What _type_ of "spirit" will generally harass the person who is inordinately sensitive and has a stronghold built around a damaged sense of self-worth?

_____

_____

40. If the permanent answer to breaking bondages does not lie in binding evil spirits, what does it lie in?

_____

_____

41. You will become better equipped spiritually through all of your prayers and warfare by using the keys of binding and loosing. What two things will you be able to more clearly discern when confronted with an evil spirit in another person?

_____

_____

_____

_____

42. What will happen if the source of vulnerability in the human soul is not dealt with?

_____

_____

_____

_____

43. When you are confronted with evil spirits, if you are always "prayed up," walking in His will, and filled daily with His Word, the Holy Spirit will direct you to do what possible things according to His guidance?

_____

_____

_____

_____

## Binding the Strong Man

44. Matthew 12:28-29 (KJV) says:

_____

_____

_____

_____

_____

_____

45. Luke 11:20-22 (KJV) says:

_____

_____

_____

_____

_____

_____

46. The right to permanently bind Satan is reserved for _____ and

_____ .

47. The verses about the strong man obviously do, however, imply that we can restrain Satan from preventing us from reclaiming and recovering what he has stolen from God's people. True or false?

48. Three steps to recovering from Satan what he has stolen are:

a) _____
b) _____
c) _____

49. To expose Satan and expose his workings, you employ two factors—what are they?

a) _____
b) _____

50. Isaiah 53:12 (KJV) tells us:

_____

_____

_____

_____

_____

_____

51. Isaiah 53:12 (KJV) is related to Luke 11:22 (NIV). The Greek word for "divide" (as used here in Luke) is _____ which means:

_____

_____

_____

_____

The word "spoils," from the Greek word _____, means _____ .

52. What did Jesus say we would do in John 14:12-14?

_____

_____


## Old Testament Confirmation

53. In Isaiah 49:25 (KJV), what does the Lord say to us?

_____

_____

_____

_____

In this passage, the Hebrew word interpreted as "mighty" is _____,
meaning: _____, _____,
_____, and also _____.

The Hebrew word interpreted as "terrible" is _____, meaning:
_____, _____, _____, _____,
_____, _____, _____, _____.

54. 1 John 3:8 (KJV) says:

_____

_____

_____

_____

_____

_____

# Chapter 4 - Review

**The most significant truths I found in this chapter are:**

1. _____
_____
_____

2. _____
_____
_____

3. _____
_____
_____

4. _____
_____
_____

**I applied these truths to my life as follows:**

1. _____
_____
_____

2. _____
_____
_____

3. _____
_____
_____

4. _____
_____
_____

# Chapter 4 - "Journey" Journal

**Date:**                         **Questions I have:**

**Date:**                         **Special insights I believe I have learned:**

**Date:**                         **Breakthroughs I have experienced:**

# Chapter 4 - Prayer Journal

**Date:**               **Prayer:**

**Date:**               **Updates and special encouragements I've received from the Lord:**

**Date:**               **Answers to prayers:**

# 5
# Loosing

## Demolishing Strongholds and Bondages

1. What do you see as the main point of the story of "Sherry"?

_____
_____
_____
_____
_____
_____

## The Bottom Line

2. A full, theologically _____ _____ of this type of praying is
_____ _____ before you will see God move to meet what you
set in motion.

3. Who is responsible for your reactions? _____

4. What can you do with the reactions you have had in the past?

_____
_____
_____
_____

5. What can you loose as you face your reactions from the past and fear rears its ugly head?

_____
_____
_____
_____

6.  If you have bound yourself to His will and purposes and you believe He has done so in heaven, what can you trust about what then begins to happen?

_____

_____

_____

_____

## Dealing With Memories That Deceive

7.  What did the author conclude when her prayers did not stop the old negative feelings she had about herself?

_____

_____

8.  What was the truth she did not realize at the time?

_____

_____

9.  You cannot loose, dissolve, or melt the unpleasant "facts" of your past, but what can you do?

_____

_____

_____

_____

10. How do you neutralize the ability of your unhappy memories to harm you?  What finally happens to them?

_____

_____

_____

_____

## No Holy Amnesia

11. In the past, you may had felt you had rid yourself of your bad memories. What do you now believe has really happened to them?

_____

_____

_____

_____

12. Who are the two spiritual beings who know every bad thing that has ever happened to you?

a) _____

b) _____

13. What are the first steps you must take before you start to loose the layers over these bad memories? Why must these steps be taken?

_____

_____

14. The _____ is where the _____ and _____ must come from—the _____ gives you _____, and allows no _____ for _____ . God's _____ _____ casts out _____ .

15. After you have used the binding side of prayer, what do you loose regarding bad memories?

_____

_____

_____

_____

16. Do you feel you are resisting God in any areas?  If so, what do you think those areas are?

_____

_____

_____

_____

17. What is your past's only function?

_____

_____

18. The author shares some of the things she began to see as she used the binding and loosing keys.  What are some of the things you have seen beginning to happen as a result of your own efforts to use these keys of the Kingdom?

_____

_____

_____

_____

## Our Spiritual Weapons

19. 2 Corinthians 10:4-5 (KJV) says: "… *the* _____ *of our* _____ *are not* _____, *but* _____ *through* _____ *to the* _____ *down of* _____ . *Casting down* _____, *and every* _____ _____ *that* _____ _____ *against the* _____ *of* _____, *and bringing into* _____ *every* _____ *to the* _____ *of* _____ ."

20. The weapons to tear down what is defeating us will never permanently come from the sources that society has learned to turn to.  What are these sources?

_____

_____

_____

_____

21. There are several ways strongholds are established—list three of them:

a) _____

b) _____

c) _____

22. The author is fully aware of a level of satanic strongholds that do need to be addressed at times.  Why has the focus of this book been kept on personal strongholds within the individual?

_____

_____

What powerful angel experienced dealing with these other issues in the Book of Daniel?

_____

_____

23. If you have personal strongholds, how effective do you think your spiritual warfare prayers will be in dealing with principalities and powers and rulers in high places?

_____

_____

24. The sources of personal strongholds can be categorized into two areas.  What are they?

a) _____

b) _____

25. The first area consists of seven sources of _____ influence.  What are they?

a) _____

b) _____

c) _____

d) _____

e) _____

f) _____

g) _____

26. The second area consists of two sources of _____ influence.  What are they?

a) _____  b) _____

27. The above influences are attracted to and protected in what part of your nature?

_____

_____

_____

_____

## Crucifying the Old Nature

28. What does the Bible tell us to crucify?

_____

_____

29. According to the Scripture, Galatians 5:16, 24-25 (TAB), what are we supposed to do?
*"Walk and live habitually in* _____ *—responsive to and*
*controlled and* _____ *by* _____ *... those who belong to Christ*
*Jesus, the Messiah, have* _____ *the flesh—the godless* _____
_____ *,—with its* _____ *and* _____ *and*
_____ *. If we live by* _____ _____ *, let us also*
*walk by* _____ *—if by the* _____ _____ *, we*
*have our* _____ _____ *, let us go* _____ *walking*
*in* _____ *, our* _____ _____ *by*
_____ *."*

30. What are the obvious things we Christians give up first to obey the Scriptures?

_____

_____

31. What do we generally employ to get these habits under control?

_____

_____

32. Where are the internal sources of wrong behaviors found?

_____

_____

33. What does the old nature do when it is left to its own devices?

_____

_____

34. Can there still be strongholds lurking within even though the external behavior seems to prove otherwise?

_____

_____

## Attitudes

35. *Webster's Dictionary* (1946) defines attitude as an instinctive mental reaction that reveals an _____ . *Webster's Dictionary* (1977) defines attitude as a mental position or feeling toward something or a _____ _____ for a _____ _____ . The media of the nineties "describes" attitude as _____ , _____ , _____ and _____ .

36. What are the attitudes we as Christians should strive to convey and where are they found?

_____

_____

37. List them:

_____ , _____ , _____ ,

_____ , _____ , _____ ,

_____ , _____ , _____ .

38. *"Those who belong to Christ Jesus have crucified the _____ _____ with its _____ and _____ . Since we live by the _____ , let us keep in step with the _____ . Let us not become _____ , provoking and _____ each other."*

39. How can we begin to accomplish this?

_____

_____

40. What are some of the wrong attitudes we can loose?

_____

_____

## Wrong Patterns of Thinking

41. Pattern means (among other things) the _____ _____ to make a _____ into which _____ _____ is poured to _____ a _____ .

42. How will anything you have poured into such a mold come out?

_____

_____

43. When wrong mind sets (patterns of thinking) are locked into place in our minds, what will come out the same way every time?

_____

_____

44. A person offended by nearly everyone is usually reacting to what?

_____

_____

45. What might someone who has been badly mistreated interpret from others' actions or words?

_____

_____

46. What protects these patterns? _____

47. Who gains access to them in order to distort and twist them even further?

_____

_____

48. How might someone who has been abused by people in power view authority?

_____

_____

49. An example of the belief of persecution used by the author is the L.A. riots of April, 1992. What are the three areas mentioned that contributed to the riot?

a) _____

b) _____

c) _____

50. Any pattern of thinking that cannot be verified with Christ-like thinking in the Word of God will always bring _____ . What are some of the examples used? Can you think of more examples?

_____

_____

51. Since facts cannot be loosed, how do we get rid of our negative feelings about what has actually happened to us?

_____

_____

52. A typical pattern of layering will follow a cruel, unfair happening in a life that is not surrendered to the will and purposes of God. This layering occurs in the following steps:

Something traumatic happens in my life which is a _____ —>

which leads me to develop a _____ —>

which helps me justify a _____ —>

which causes me to erect a _____ to protect my right to do so —>

which _____ my _____ by _____ the

_____ _____ in and _____ _____ out.

53. You cannot loose the fact of the original trauma or abuse, but you can:

_____
_____
_____
_____

What do you bind and loose in this situation?

_____
_____
_____
_____

54. What are you trying to expose and why?

_____
_____

55. When your mind begins to search for protection as the "layers" come off, what is necessary for you to bind?

_____
_____

## Ideas

56. What do your ideas represent?

_____
_____
_____
_____

57. What words, in the KJV, are closest to the English word "idea"?

_____
_____

58. 2 Corinthians 10:4-5 speaks of a need for:

_____
_____
_____

59. What are we doing when we loose wrong ideas?

_____
_____
_____
_____

## Desires

60. *Webster's Dictionary* defines ''desire'' as:

_____
_____
_____
_____

61. In the original Greek text, the word ''desire'' is described as:

_____
_____

62. Where do wrong desires comes from?

_____
_____

63. You can't loose an unmet need, but what can you loose to open the way to getting that need met?

_____
_____

64. How is the "acting out" of a need often perceived by others?

_____
_____

65. How does the needy person often begin to perceive their own unmet needs?

_____
_____

66. When an unmet need exists, it exerts internal pressure that manifests itself in what external form?

_____
_____

67. Who is the only one who can fulfill and satisfy our unmet needs?

_____
_____

68. What are some examples of wrong desires and their resulting issues?

_____
_____
_____
_____
_____
_____

## Beliefs

69. A belief is the mental:

_____

_____

70. A Christian's right beliefs fortify and strengthen his or her faith which is:

_____

_____

_____

_____

(Hebrews 11:9, KJV)

71. What does our trust in wrong beliefs turn into?

_____

_____

72. What will sustained faith in a wrong belief do?

_____

_____

73. Loosing wrong beliefs does not mean they will automatically disappear. What will they no longer be able to do when you have loosed them? Why?

_____

_____

74. What do you do when you reject wrong beliefs?

_____

_____

75. As you loose a wrong belief, what must you bind yourself to?

_____

_____

## Behaviors and Habits

76. A behavior is:

_____

_____

A habit is:

_____

_____

77. What does negative motivation actually do?

_____

_____

78. What does behavior modification actually do?

_____

_____

79. What is the better solution to uncovering destructive behavior patterns?

_____

_____

80. What can stress, pain, and guilt stimulate?

_____

_____

81. Fear of being controlled can stimulate:

_____

_____

82. Unmet needs can stimulate:

_____

_____

83. How do you make room within yourself for the restoration work of the Holy Spirit?

_____

_____

84. What will you be able to receive if you have submitted your body, mind, will, and emotions to the will and purposes of God?

_____

_____

85. Why must sins and strongholds be destroyed?

_____

_____

## Whatsoever—A Very Big Word

86. Only God knows where His plan for your life may take you. What does this have to do with what you should or should not bind yourself to?

_____

_____

87. What will sticking to these guidelines keep you from getting into conflict with?

_____

_____

88. What is the true test of a new spiritual understanding?

_____

_____

_____

_____

# Chapter 5 - Review

**The most significant truths I found in this chapter are:**

**1.** _____

_____

_____

**2.** _____

_____

_____

**3.** _____

_____

_____

**4.** _____

_____

_____

**I applied these truths to my life as follows:**

1. _____

_____

_____

**2.** _____

_____

_____

**3.** _____

_____

_____

**4.** _____

_____

_____

# Chapter 5 - "Journey" Journal

**Date:**                    **Questions I have:**

**Date:**                    **Special insights I believe I have learned:**

**Date:**                    **Breakthroughs I have experienced:**

# Chapter 5 - Prayer Journal

**Date:**             **Prayer:**

**Date:**             **Updates and special encouragements I've received from the Lord:**

**Date:**             **Answers to prayers:**

# 6
# Forgiving and Repenting

1.  You cannot buy true forgiveness, it is given as a gift—but is God's forgiveness really unconditional?  Explain your answer.

_____

_____

_____

_____

2.  There are four Scriptures referenced in the opening of this chapter regarding "conditions" for receiving the gift of forgiveness—Matthew 6:12,14-15 (KJV), Mark 11:25 (NIV), Ephesians 4:32 (KJV), and Colossians 3:13 (NIV).  Please write the "key" phrase or words that illustrate the "conditions" in each Scripture:

Matthew 6:12,14-15 (KJV)

_____

_____

Mark 11:25 (NIV)

_____

_____

Ephesians 4:32 (KJV)

_____

_____

Colossians 3:13 (NIV)

_____

_____

The conclusion is that we receive God's forgiveness in exactly the same manner that we:

_____

_____

3. What can severely complicate our ability to forgive others?

_____

_____

4. What can forgiveness on your part do to your old hurts?

_____

_____

5. What is it time to start doing when God asks you to do something you are convinced that you cannot do?

_____

_____

6. Being very forgiving of all the easy things to forgive can help you deny that you have not forgiven some of the hard things. True or False?

7. What good thing can you turn your pain into?

_____

_____

8. 1 Peter 2:23-24 (TAB) says: *"When He (Jesus) was _____ and _____, He did not _____ or offer _____ in return; when He was _____ and _____, He made no _____ of _____; but He _____ himself and _____ to Him who _____ _____ . He personally _____ our _____ in His own body to the tree as to an altar and _____ himself on it that we might _____ (cease to exist) to _____ and _____ to _____ . By His _____ you have been _____ ."*

9. The author states:

"Jesus entrusted everything to His Father who judges fairly and then made provision for us through His own wounds. If we refuse to revile, insult or threaten vengeance when we are wounded, we allow His wounds to heal us and others?" How do we walk in this attitude?

_____

_____

_____

_____

10. 1 Peter 3:9-11 (TAB) says:

_____

_____

_____

_____

11. How or why can we glory in our tribulations (Romans 5:3-4, KJV)?

_____

_____

_____

_____

12. The Greek word for "experience" means:

_____

_____

13. What kind of faith is untried, untested, untempered faith?

_____

_____

14. Why is faith given to you (according to the text of *Shattering Your Strongholds)*?

_____

_____

15. How do you become more like fine gold?

_____

_____

_____

_____

16. How would you express Romans 5 in your own words of prayer to our heavenly Father?

_____

_____

_____

_____

## Dealing With Anger

17. If anger is never an acceptable response to a personal affront, why do you suppose God created us with a capacity for anger?

_____

_____

_____

_____

18. How long does the Scriptures say we have to resolve our anger at anyone or anything?

_____

_____

_____

_____

19. According to Ephesians 4:26-27 (TAB), what did Jesus say about anger?

_____

_____

_____

_____

20. What is your most powerful first line of attack when you feel indignant, your pride is offended, or you think you have been wronged?

_____

_____

21. In your own words, what would you pray based on the words of Psalm 119:165 and Proverbs 16:18, when pride has become an issue in your life?

_____

_____

_____

_____

_____

_____

## The Things God Hates

22. Proverbs 6:16 (KJV) says: *"These six things doth the Lord hate: yea, seven are an abomination to him . . . ."* What are the seven things God hates?

a)  A _____ _____ .

b)  A _____ _____ .

c)  Hands that _____ _____ _____ .

d)  An heart that _____ _____ _____ .

e)  Feet that be _____ in _____ to _____ .

f)  A _____ _____ that _____ _____ .

g)  He that _____ _____ among the _____ .

23. When pride, anger, hurt feelings, etc. seem to have almost a stranglehold on you, how can you break that hold and bring them and your situation to the Lord in prayer?

_____

_____

_____

_____

## Who's Going to Pay?

24. Give an example of a subtle payback in response to an offense:

_____

_____

_____

_____

Have you ever employed subtle paybacks in your Christian life?_____

How can you avoid that in the future?

_____

_____

25. The "world's" solution to an affront is: "Somebody will pay for this!" In your own words, why is this not appropriate for a blood-bought child of God?

_____

_____

26. What is revenge?

_____

_____

27. Whose responsibility is it to retaliate when a wrong has been inflicted on you?

_____

_____

28. Romans 12:17-19 (KJV) says:

_____

_____

_____

_____

## Our Struggle With Forgiveness

29. Define "forgiving" according to *Webster's Dictionary*.

_____

_____

What did *Webster's Dictionary* leave out?

_____

_____

30. When you forgive, do you believe you have accomplished forgiveness based on feeling? Give a reason for your answer, whether yes or no:

_____

_____

_____

_____

31. How can you know when you have forgiven someone?

_____

_____

_____

_____

32. What does true forgiveness do to a bad memory?

_____

_____

33. When you have continually forgiven the same offense, how many times did Jesus say you should keep on forgiving?

_____

_____

34. Which of the binding and loosing keys can you employ in a situation where forgiveness is so hard that it takes an act of the will over and over again to forgive?

_____

_____

35. What did Jesus say in Matthew 6:14-15 (TAB)?

_____

_____

_____

_____

_____

_____

_____

36. God will forgive a wrong state of heart when that heart surrenders to Him and seeks to be restored to a right state. If a heart steadfastly refuses to forgive, God will not forgive the state of that heart. When you refuse to forgive, what are you cutting yourself off from?

_____

_____

_____

_____

37. What is probably a real problem for you if you believe God has not really forgiven you?

_____

_____

38. What will someone most likely do who has known little forgiveness and grace while growing up?

_____

_____

39. What might cause you to bitterly defend your right to not forgive?

_____

_____

_____

_____

## Avoiding the Tormentors

40. In your own words, what does Matthew 18:23-35 say to you?

_____

_____

_____

_____

_____

_____

41. How can we jeopardize our own forgiveness?

_____

_____

42. How do we become more susceptible to the will of the tormentors?

_____

_____

43. The original Greek word and its associated words that mean "tormentor" translate as five types. What are they?

a) _____

b) _____

c) _____

d) _____

e) _____

44. Who are these beings that you listed above?

_____

_____

45. What are some of the other names for these tormentors?

_____

_____

_____

_____

46. What are some things that the stronghold protecting unforgiveness will block?

_____

_____

_____

_____

_____

47. How can you unknowingly release chemical poisons into your body?

_____

_____

## Nothing Can Replace Forgiveness

48. There are many misconceptions about what does and does not constitute an act of forgiveness.  Mark out the incorrect words in the following list:

    Forgiveness  is/is not  tolerance towards an offense
    Forgiveness  is/is not  being able to pretend nothing happened
    Forgiveness  is/is not  a deliberate act of the will
    Forgiveness  is/is not  an act of forgetting
    Forgiveness  is/is not  key to full freedom
    Forgiveness  is/is not  turning the other cheek
    Forgiveness  is/is not  looking the other way
    Forgiveness  is/is not  an act of love
    Forgiveness  is/is not  politeness
    Forgiveness  is/is not  obedience to the Word of God
    Forgiveness  is/is not  diplomacy
    Forgiveness  is/is not  a passive non-response
    Forgiveness  is/is not  a full pardon
    Forgiveness  is/is not  generosity of spirit
    Forgiveness  is/is not  a substitutional act

49. The first part of Hebrews 4:12 (KJV) says:  *"For the word of God is quick (alive), and powerful, and sharper than any two-edged sword, piercing even to the dividing asunder of soul and spirit . . . ."*  What is the author's interpretative comment here?

_____

_____

_____

_____

The second part of Hebrews 4:12 (KJV) says: "*. . . and of the joints and marrow, and is a discerner of the thoughts and intents of the heart.*" What is the author's interpretative comment here?

_____

_____

Do you agree with these comments? _____ Why?

_____

_____

_____

_____

50. Forgiveness is not forgetting a wrong. You "forget" the hurt only _____ you

_____ .

51. When you do not forgive, what happens to your feelings? Where do they go?

_____

_____

52. When bitterness drips into your inner being, what happens?

_____

_____

---

**Have you experienced this in your own life? Recall a still-painful incident from your past. Determine to use the tools you have learned to forgive and ask forgiveness if that person is alive.**

---

53. Strongholds of _____ and _____ are like _____ _____ and _____ that _____ _____ in your _____ . Once established, they will _____ the _____ out of your _____ _____ , your _____ _____ , your _____ , your _____ and your _____ to _____ . Roots of bitterness cause _____ in your _____ , setting up _____ _____ which the enemy then _____ to _____ you _____ .

54. The writer of Hebrews says in 6:7-8 (NIV): "*Land that drinks in the rain often falling on it and that produces a crop useful to those for whom it is farmed receives the* _____ *of* _____ . *But land that produces* _____ *and* _____ *is* _____ *and is in* _____ *of being* _____ . *In the end it will be* _____ ."

55. Hebrews 12:15 (NIV) says: "*See to it that no one* _____ *the* _____ *of* _____ *and that no* _____ _____ *grows up to cause* _____ *and* _____ _____ .*"

## The Cost of Forgiveness

56. What does our old nature want to do with an offense?

_____

_____

57. Forgiveness denies our _____ _____ any
_____ to cry out for _____, _____ and
_____ of what we have suffered at the hands of another.

Forgiveness denies our _____ to protect our _____, to
_____ and _____ it and _____ it around for all
to see.

Forgiveness denies our _____ to tell our _____
_____.

58. Forgiveness says we will _____ the _____ for the other
_____ _____ .

59. What did Jesus use to pay the "full price" for our sins?

_____

_____

60. What must you be to become part of the Bride of Christ?

_____

_____

61. What is often in the heart of those in the world who are very casual about saying they
forgive?

_____

_____

_____

_____

62. Real forgiveness is not:

_____

_____

What makes it costly to the one who forgives?

_____

_____

63. Forgiveness is a matter of _____ _____ or
_____ .

64. What can you do if old memories return to haunt you?

_____

_____

## God Will Take Care of the Details

65. 1 Peter 2:23 (NIV) says: *"When they hurled their insults at him, he did not*
_____*; when he suffered, he* _____ *no* _____ *.*
*Instead, he* _____ *himself to him who* _____ _____
*."*

66. What is the message the world sends and our old nature embraces with a vengeance?

_____

_____

67. The debt we owed God was so enormous that it was beyond anyone's ability to pay except God himself. So God came to us in the form of Christ to pay our debt on the cross with His own blood.

<u>Have you accepted</u> the fact that Christ bore your sins on the cross?
<u>Have you accepted</u> that He paid a debt you owed, but you could never repay?
<u>Have you accepted</u> His all-inclusive, total sacrifice for your forgiveness and freedom?

Can you honestly say that you have truly settled these questions in your own heart?

If not, you need to do so right now. Use your binding and loosing keys to bind yourself to God's will, the blood of Christ, and the truth. Then loose deception and wrong beliefs and strongholds from yourself. Loose word curses, generational bondages, and religious bondages from yourself. By the words of your mouth, speak out in faith and accept His forgiveness, His love, and His mercy and grace.

68. What will society promote and what nature does it appeal to?

_____

_____

_____

_____

_____

69. What is the world's greed always ready to feed on?

_____

_____

70. How many does it generally take to work out forgiveness in your life? Who are they?

_____

_____

_____

_____

71. You don't have to resolve the forgiveness issue all by yourself—God is willing to help you.  True or false?

72. Phillipians 2:13 (NIV) says: *"It is _____ who _____ in _____ to _____ and to _____ according to _____ _____ _____."*

# Chapter 6 - Review

**The most significant truths I found in this chapter are:**

1. _____
   _____
   _____

2. _____
   _____
   _____

3. _____
   _____
   _____

4. _____
   _____
   _____

**I applied these truths to my life as follows:**

1. _____
   _____
   _____

2. _____
   _____
   _____

3. _____
   _____
   _____

4. _____
   _____
   _____

# Chapter 6 - "Journey" Journal

**Date:**                               **Questions I have:**

**Date:**                               **Special insights I believe I have learned:**

**Date:**                               **Breakthroughs I have experienced:**

# Chapter 6 - Prayer Journal

**Date:**                 **Prayer:**

**Date:**                 **Updates and special encouragements I've received from the Lord:**

**Date:**                 **Answers to prayers:**

# 7
# Setting Yourself Free

## Using Your Keys

> ## Key Statement:
> It is very important to apply these keys to yourself
> before using them to pray for others.

1.  What happens when you neglect praying for your own spiritual needs and strength?
_____
_____
_____
_____

2.  What else must you do when you pray?

_____
_____

3.  What will increase as you bind yourself to the will of God and the truth, and loose the former things of your old nature and its strongholds?

_____
_____

## Daily Preparations

4.  Review your spiritual armor:

a)  <u>Loins girded,</u> (bound about) with truth;
b)  <u>Breastplate of righteousness</u> (bound to your chest);
c)  <u>Feet shod</u> (tied around) with the preparation of the gospel of peace;
d)  <u>Shield of faith</u> (joined to one hand);
e)  <u>Helmet of salvation</u> (fastened over) on your head;
f)  The <u>sword of the Spirit</u> (held in the other hand).

The words in parentheses (on the previous page) are the various meanings of Greek words for _____ .

5.  Cite four "key phrases" from four of the Scriptures listed that tell us why it is important to apply our armor every day:

a) _____

b) _____

c) _____

d) _____

## Working Out Your Own Salvation

6.  Our understanding of spiritual things is to be an ongoing, _____ pattern of _____, _____, and _____ .

7.  What is another reason to reinforce your spiritual armor daily?

_____

_____

8.  How can you relate the manna (that God gave to the Israelites each day) to your spiritual walk?

_____

_____

_____

_____

9.  What does Solomon say in Proverbs 24:10?

_____

_____

_____

_____

10. What does God load us with on a daily basis?  Are <u>you</u> receiving these things daily?  If not, do you know why?

_____

_____

_____

_____

11. What keeps us from playing the old "what's wrong with this picture" game?

_____

_____

_____

_____

12. Did you receive a complete work of restoration the moment you confessed your faith?

_____

_____

13. How can we speed up the process of restoration in our life?

_____

_____

## Quick Trip to Calvary

14. Philippians 2:5 (KJV) says:

_____

_____

15. Is the natural mind of man able to receive the things of God?

_____

_____

16. What is the fastest way to accomplish the crucifixion of your old nature?

_____

_____

17. What must we do to receive our transformed, renewed mind?

_____

_____

_____

_____

18. Does Christ force unity with Him upon us?  What must we do to achieve it?

_____

_____

_____

_____

19. What are some of the Christian cliches that are used often and that can leave a struggling Christian feeling even worse?

_____

_____

_____

_____

20. What is a practical way you can achieve "letting go and letting God"?

_____

_____

21. Why do the answers seem to elude us, especially when the Word of God says they are ours to receive?

_____

_____

22. Strongholds can become so impenetrable that nothing gets in unless it fits what?

_____

_____

23. What do we often do even when we don't want to?

_____

_____

## Releasing Misconceptions

24. Even if we have a desire to surrender to the Lord, what will keep us resisting that surrender?

_____

_____

25. What kind of heart will respond to God's every wish?

_____

_____

26. What is a natural outflow of a heart cleansed by misconceptions of the old nature?

_____

_____

_____

_____

27. Why might we cling to misconceptions?

_____

_____

_____

_____

28. Ephesians 4:22-24 (TAB) states:

_____

_____

_____

_____

_____

_____

29. What is the order in this Scripture regarding your two natures?

_____

_____

_____

_____

30. What will you give up when you bind your mind to the mind of Christ?  Are you ready to do that?  If you have already been doing that, what do you see has happened regarding patterns and attitudes?

_____

_____

_____

_____

## Making Room

31. What must we be able to do in order to be fulfilled and to become an overcomer?

_____

_____

32. How far can Jesus come into your "house"?  Is there ample room so that He can bring anything in with Him?

_____

_____

_____

_____

33. In all truthfulness, is Jesus a resident in your house, or is He just an honored guest?

_____

_____

34. What factors do our spirit, soul, and body come in contact with every day?

_____

_____

_____

_____

_____

35. What happens when you have a partially surrendered mind?

_____

_____

_____

_____

36. In your own condensed words, how can you pray for yourself to strip away the old things of your old nature?

_____

_____

_____

_____

## Word Curses

37. How do spoken words have the power to affect us?

_____

_____

38. Psalm 109:3 (KJV) says, *"They compassed me about also with _____ of _____ ."*

39. Proverbs 18:8 (KJV) says, *"The _____ of a talebearer are as _____ ."*

40. After harsh words have been spoken to you, what will usually bring peace?

_____

_____

_____

_____

41. What was one of the strongest confirmations the author had that the personal application of the keys to her old nature had achieved success?

_____

_____

_____

_____

42. What can reactivate word curses against you and, therefore, needs to be dealt with accordingly?

_____

_____

_____

_____

Satan inflames _____ when old natures are filled with strongholds protecting unmet needs and unresolved pain. This can cause us or others to do what?

_____

_____

## The Magnitude of Words Spoken

43. How can wrong words have an impact in your life?

_____

_____

_____

_____

44. How can you protect yourself from wrong words being spoken about you?

_____

_____

_____

_____

## Right Words

45. How do we practice the words of God?

_____

_____

_____

_____

_____

_____

_____

46. Romans 10:8 (KJV) says:

_____

_____

_____

_____

_____

Circle what you consider to be <u>key words</u> in this Scripture.

47. Romans 10:10 says:

_____

_____

_____

Circle what you consider to be the <u>key words </u>in this Scripture.

48. James 3:9-10 (NIV) says:

_____

_____

_____

_____

Circle what you consider to be the <u>key words</u> in this Scripture.

49. What can you do if you have spoken word curses about others?

_____

_____

_____

_____

50. What can you do if you have spoken word curses about your children?

_____

_____

_____

_____

_____

51. How would you pray the words in Psalm 103:17? Write out your prayer here.

_____

_____

_____

_____

52. In your own words, how would you pray the words of God in Isaiah 49:24-25? Write out your prayer here.

_____

_____

_____

_____

53. What are some of the word curses you might be pronouncing on yourself as you struggle to make your economic "ends" meet?

_____

_____

_____

_____

54. What are some of the things you might loose to break the power and effects of those words?

_____

_____

_____

_____

55. How might you pray the words of 2 Corinthians 9:6-8? Write out your prayer here.

_____

_____

_____

_____

## Generational Bondages

56. What does Exodus 20:5 say about generational bondages?

_____

_____

_____

_____

_____

57. What are some bondages that can be passed from generation to generation?

_____

_____

_____

_____

58. Because of strongholds, what may cause believers to be held down and held back?

_____

_____

_____

_____

59. Why do many belivers doubt they are subject to generational bondages?

_____

_____

_____

_____

60. What can keep believers from living in liberty and abundant life?

_____

_____

_____

_____

61. What can unresolved pain and bitterness create in your life?

_____

_____

62. What do you consider the most important line in the "training wheel prayers" on pages 139 to 141 of *Shattering Your Strongholds*?

_____

_____

_____

_____

63. Is it necessary to mention specific strongholds or specific patterns hindering you when you pray?

_____

_____

64. The author lists several things you will become aware of as you begin praying this way— what are some of the ways she mentions?

_____

_____

_____

_____

_____

_____

65. What are some of the things you have become aware of in your life after studying this chapter?

_____

_____

_____

_____

_____

_____

# Chapter 7 - Review

**The most significant truths I found in this chapter are:**

1.  _____
    _____
    _____

2.  _____
    _____
    _____

3.  _____
    _____
    _____

4.  _____
    _____
    _____

**I applied these truths to my life as follows:**

1.  _____
    _____
    _____

2.  _____
    _____
    _____

3.  _____
    _____
    _____

4.  _____
    _____
    _____

# Chapter 7 - "Journey" Journal

**Date:**                    **Questions I have:**

**Date:**                    **Special insights I believe I have learned:**

**Date:**                    **Breakthroughs I have experienced:**

# Chapter 7 - Prayer Journal

**Date:**                **Prayer:**

**Date:**                **Updates and special encouragements I've received from the Lord:**

**Date:**                **Answers to prayers:**

# 8
# Sarah's Story

1. Matthew 18:18-20 (KJV) says: *"Verily I say unto you, _____ ye shall _____ on earth shall be bound in _____; and _____ ye shall _____ on earth shall be loosed in heaven. Again I say unto you, That if _____ of you shall _____ on earth as touching _____ _____ that they shall _____, it shall be _____ for them of my Father which is in heaven. For where _____ or _____ are gathered together in _____ _____, there am I in the _____ of _____."*

2. How do some use this verse? How has the author applied this verse?

_____
_____
_____
_____

What is the one truth that probably all Christians can agree on about praying with others?

_____
_____

## Lab Rats in the Prayer Laboratory

3. Why do you think the author called her intercessory prayer group a prayer laboratory? What does that terminology mean to you?

_____
_____
_____
_____
_____

4.  Regarding the binding and loosing prayers and the covenant contained in Matthew 16:19 and Matthew 18:18, what can we know even though the answers to our prayers have not fully come?

_____

_____

_____

_____

## Prayers of Confusion

5.  What were the probable causes and resulting behaviors involved in the dynamics of the relationship between Sarah and her mother?

Sarah's mother:

_____

_____

_____

_____

Sarah:

_____

_____

_____

_____

6.  What was one powerful stronghold they both held in common?  What does this stronghold generally do to people, and what is the ultimate destruction it can effect?

_____

_____

_____

_____

_____

_____

## Prayers of Power

7.  Name some of the things the author and Sarah's mother began <u>to bind Sarah to</u> and <u>loose from Sarah</u>?

_____

_____

_____

_____

Special Note: According to the author's understanding of what the Holy Spirit taught her to bind, you bind yourself to the good and stable attributes and things of God. You loose wrong things from yourself and from others. So many were loosing themselves and people from things, the "splinter principle" of loosing (not in the book) was introduced to help clarify that point. When you are trying to remove a splinter from your hand, you do not loose or remove your hand from the splinter—you loose or remove the splinter from your hand. The most effective application of the loosing key is to loose the destructive, offending, hindering, pain-causing "splinter" from the person.

## Strongholds Broken

8. Binding and loosing prayers helped destroy the strongholds the _____ had been able to access. The _____ for their _____ had been broken and the _____ for Sarah's _____ had been laid.

## God's Perfect Timing

9. Once the human body has depleted its store of fat and muscle in a case of extreme anorexia, what does it normally begin to eat next? What is a frequent occurence in the case of near starvation?

_____
_____
_____
_____

## Time Frames/Reunion Time in Arizona

10. Deliverance is often a process that requires a time frame we do not always understand. Why does God sometimes allow time to elapse before a deliverance or healing is manifested?

_____
_____
_____
_____
_____

11. What is one of Sarah's most powerful personal factors in her testimony?

_____
_____
_____
_____

## Teaching From Experience

12. In your own words, what do you think is the most compelling factor in the difference between teaching from actual experience and teaching from pure knowledge and theory?

_____

_____

_____

_____

13. How can we speed up the process of restoration in our life?

_____

_____

_____

_____

## Destroying the Enemy's Works

14. Why did God tell the armies of Israel to destroy all the possessions of their enemy after a victory over them—even down to the women and children?

_____

_____

15. When you are involved in a battle with your enemy, the author says, "Through the power of loosing, destroy even what seems to be harmless." Can you list at least three things in your own life that appeared to be harmless, yet eventually turned into snares and traps?

_____

_____

_____

_____

16. When we use the powerful key of loosing here on earth, by the words of our mouth, what can we count on God's reaction to be?

_____

_____

17. Read the Scriptures on page 161 of *Shattering Your Strongholds,* (Psalm 18:32-42, KJV). Can you list at least four references in these ten verses that agree with the meanings of the original Greek and Hebrew words for loosing (found in Chapters 4 and 5)?

_____

_____

_____

_____

18. What is a major factor in the difference between victory and defeat in our spiritual warfare?

_____

_____

19. Explain the out-of-sight/out-of-mind mentality with regard to spiritual warfare.

_____

_____

_____

_____

What can result if you "buy into" this mentality/mind set/attitude?

_____

_____

_____

_____

20. In your own words, describe what you learned from Sarah's story:

_____

_____

_____

_____

_____

_____

_____

_____

_____

_____

_____

_____

21. The final point (#7) of the summary for this chapter says: "A consistent and persistent tenacity is crucial for victory in spiritual warfare."

Describe what this statement means to you. Give an example of standing fast to hold the line against the enemy or describe an actual event in your life where you personally achieved victory through "consistent and persistent" warfare.

_____

_____

_____

_____

_____

_____

_____

In your own words, write a short prayer you might pray based on your favorite Scripture for standing fast, holding your ground, and pressing into a problem (rather than retreating from it).

_____

_____

_____

_____

_____

_____

_____

_____

_____

_____

# Chapter 8 - Review

**The most significant truths I found in this chapter are:**

**1.** _____
_____
_____

**2.** _____
_____
_____

**3.** _____
_____
_____

**4.** _____
_____
_____

**I applied these truths to my life as follows:**

1. _____
_____
_____

2. _____
_____
_____

3. _____
_____
_____

4. _____
_____
_____

# Chapter 8 - "Journey" Journal

**Date:**                    **Questions I have:**

**Date:**                    **Special insights I believe I have learned:**

**Date:**                    **Breakthroughs I have experienced:**

# Chapter 8 - Prayer Journal

**Date:**                    Prayer:

**Date:**                    Updates and special encouragements I've received from the Lord:

**Date:**                    Answers to prayers:

# 9

# Setting the Captives Free

## (Whether They Want to Be or Not!)

1. In addition to your loved ones, for whom else can you pray the binding and loosing prayers?  For whom else <u>have</u> you prayed them?

_____
_____
_____
_____

2. Jude 21-23 (KJV) states: *"Keep yourselves in the* _____ *of* _____ *, looking for the* _____ *of our Lord Jesus Christ unto* _____ _____ *. And of some have* _____ *, making a* _____ *: And others* _____ *with* _____ *, pulling them* _____ *of the* _____ *. . . ."*

3. What helps you achieve the first part of Jude 21-23?

_____
_____

4. What is the harder part of this Scripture to comply with and to understand?

_____
_____

5. Whether or not someone wants help is not the issue here.  What is the real issue?

_____
_____

6. What is a "belief" that might cause someone to refuse security, health, liberty, love, peace, joy, or power?

_____
_____

7.  What have thousands done in hopes of receiving something from Satan?

_____

_____

8.  Name seven things that a person might experience who is captive to his or her <u>old</u> natural mind, controlled by his or her old nature:

a) _____

b) _____

c) _____

d) _____

e) _____

f) _____

g) _____

9.  Those who are held captive by their old minds are "following" what kind of script?

_____

_____

## The Right Mind

10.  The right mind:

Receives what?_____

Is capable of what? _____

Is capable of what if renewed?_____

Is a what?_____

Is also a what? _____

Has what?_____

Is the same mind as in who?_____

11.  The right mind is in unity with what?

_____

_____

12.  What does 2 Peter 1:4 (KJV) say?

_____

_____

_____

_____

_____

_____

13. Partake/partaker, when translated from the Greek, means which of the following words? Cross out those that are incorrect:

Participant, practical, compassionate, associate, capable, companion, sympathetic, fellowship, empathetic.

14. What does it mean to "surrender your thoughts to Christ"?

_____

_____

15. Concerning an unsurrendered soul that you have been praying for, what Scripture can you stand on to pray effectively for his or her surrender to Christ? And what will happen as you follow that Scripture?

_____

_____

_____

_____

## Whosoever

16. John 3:16-17 (KJV) says: *"For God so _____ the _____, that he _____ his only begotten _____, that _____ _____ in him should not _____, but have _____ _____. For God sent not his Son into the _____ to _____ the world; but that the world _____ _____ might be _____."*

17. What do you consider to be the key phrase in 2 Peter 3:9?

_____

_____

18. What do you consider to be the key phrase in 1 Timothy 2:3-4?

_____

_____

19. If Satan's will is to control the will of "whosoever," how can you best thwart his efforts?

_____

_____

20. What will Satan try to hammer and break in his desire to thwart your efforts of praying the binding and loosing prayers for your unbelieving loved ones?

_____

_____

21. What type of people are the most difficult to reach with the gospel?

_____
_____
_____
_____

22.  2 Corinthians 4:4 (KJV) says: *"The god of* _____ _____ *hath* _____ *the* _____ *of them which* _____ _____ *, lest the* _____ *of the glorious* _____ *of* _____ *, who is the* _____ *of* _____ *, should shine unto* _____ *."*

23. What kind of undertanding of the truth do those who are under this blindness have?

_____
_____
_____
_____

They don't believe they are rejecting truth.  What do they believe they are rejecting?

_____
_____

24. How do you help such a person?

_____
_____

25. How can you use this method of praying in order to intercede for a backslider?

_____
_____
_____
_____

## Spiritual Battle

26. Why is it so difficult for you to persevere in the natural regarding an unsaved loved one?

_____
_____
_____
_____

27. What kind of battle is it difficult to stay away from when you try to deal with stubbornness in the natural realm?

_____
_____

28. With what is your true battle, and where must it be fought?

_____
_____
_____
_____
_____
_____

29. How might you pray for a loved one who is stubbornly resisting the love of God?

_____
_____
_____
_____
_____
_____

30. What did the author liken to the positive and negative sides of the power of binding?

_____
_____

31. What must you do for a captive you have pulled out of the fire? Why?

_____
_____
_____
_____

32. What part of binding and loosing (stripping and tearing down) can be accomplished only by the individual himself or herself?

_____
_____
_____
_____

## Loosing the Grave Clothes

33. What are the grave clothes?

_____
_____

34. What did Jesus do about the stone at Lazarus' tomb?

_____
_____
_____
_____

35. What was Lazarus' problem when he came out of the tomb?

_____

_____

36. Who did Jesus tell to do something about that problem?  What did Jesus say to do?

_____

_____

_____

_____

## Training Wheel Prayer

37. List the seven internal sources of influence that need to be loosed:

a) _____

b) _____

c) _____

d) _____

e) _____

f) _____

g) _____

List the two external sources of influence to be loosed:

a) _____

b) _____

38. List the three most powerful (to you, personally) sentences in the training wheel prayer on pages 171 and 172.

a) _____

b) _____

c) _____

Are you aware of why these three sentences have a special appeal for you and seem to stand out more than the others do when you pray them?

_____

_____

## Reversing Parental Mistakes

39. Give an example of the sins of the parents being visited upon generation after generation.

_____

_____

40. Although you cannot erase the mistakes that you and your parents have made, what can you do to dissolve the negative effects of the bondages that have been inherited from those mistakes?

_____

_____

_____

_____

```
┌─────────────────────────────────────────────────┐
│                 Key Statement:                  │
│  As you have practiced the principles of binding and loosing in your own life, │
│     the Holy Spirit generally will have revealed specific things to you.    │
│        These may be specific attitudes and patterns of thinking         │
│           you also need to loose from your children.            │
└─────────────────────────────────────────────────┘
```

41. What can cause you to loose symptoms rather than root causes?

_____

_____

_____

_____

42. What are some of the things you can expect to see manifested as you faithfully and consistently apply the binding and loosing prayers to your family members?

_____

_____

_____

_____

## Stabilizing Your Loved Ones

43. What will happen to a person who has come to the point of deliverance through prayer and ministry if spiritual support is withdrawn from them too soon?

_____

_____

_____

44. How long do you need to continue to pray for them?

_____

_____

## Battle Behind Their Backs

45. Jesus did not say He was sent only to pray and intercede. He said He was . . . (what?):

_____

_____

_____

46. What do you consider to be the three key phrases of Isaiah 49:24-25 (KJV or NIV)?

a) _____

_____

b) _____

_____

c) _____

_____

47. How do your binding and loosing prayers affect those who are spiritually blind, and what will be the ultimate result of your warfare?

_____

_____

_____

_____

## Far-Reaching Implications

48. Write out 1 Timothy 2:1-2 and then circle the words you consider to be the key words:

_____

_____

_____

_____

49. List (by name) the leaders you need to pray for (local, county, state, national, world, other authority figures):

_____

_____

_____

_____

50. What nation should we always continue to pray for, in addition to America?

_____

_____

51. Why is it important to pray for that country and its people?

_____

_____

52. Name three powerful things God says in Isaiah 27:3-4?

a) _____
_____

b) _____
_____

c) _____
_____

53. In your own words, how might you now pray for Israel after learning the principles of the binding and loosing way of praying?

_____
_____
_____
_____
_____
_____
_____
_____

54. In your own words, how might you now pray for believers everywhere?

_____
_____
_____
_____
_____
_____
_____
_____
_____
_____

# Chapter 9 - Review

**The most significant truths I found in this chapter are:**

1. _____
_____
_____

2. _____
_____
_____

3. _____
_____
_____

4. _____
_____
_____

**I applied these truths to my life as follows:**

1. _____
_____
_____

2. _____
_____
_____

3. _____
_____
_____

4. _____
_____
_____

# Chapter 9 - "Journey" Journal

**Date:**                    **Questions I have:**

**Date:**                    **Special insights I believe I have learned:**

**Date:**                    **Breakthroughs I have experienced:**

# Chapter 9 - Prayer Journal

**Date:**                    **Prayer:**

**Date:**                    Updates and special encouragements I've received from the Lord:

**Date:**                    Answers to prayers:

# 10
# Yes, It Really Works!

1. What does the author say is the key to the contents of this book?

_____

_____

2. What is the key word in Matthew 16:19 that most Christians have seemed to ignore?

_____

_____

3. Who is man's worst enemy?

_____

_____

4. As we have run from, hidden from, and fought with Satan for years, what have we been allowing him to steal from us?

_____

_____

5. All the while, the real enemy we should be defeating has been what?

_____

_____

6. What has always been one of man's major excuses for his own failures?

_____

_____

7. God removes every opportunity for man to use that excuse after the Battle of Armegeddon.  Explain how:

_____

_____

_____

_____

8. What can Satan get that gives him power over the believer?

_____

_____

_____

_____

9. Many have used the keys of binding to bind evil spirits. This is only a

_____

_____

_____for surviving.

10. Succesful survival and victory are synonymous. True or false?

11. To what must binding and loosing be applied in order to make them function most effectively?

_____

_____

_____

_____

12. Can you continue to oppose yourself and still be an overcomer? Explain your answer:

_____

_____

_____

_____

_____

_____

13. Many are crying out for their causes and their rights in the world—some good and some bad. But individual rights not held up to the Word of God are almost always what?

_____

_____

## Jesus is the Head

14. What is Jesus supposed to be the head of?

_____

_____

15. What do 1 Corinthians 12:12 and the following verses refer to?

_____

_____

_____

_____

What is your actual understanding of Jesus being the Head and us being the body? Explain the functional comparison between the natural human body and the spiritual Body of Christ:

_____

_____

_____

_____

16. What happens to those who do not choose to make Christ their head?

_____

_____

17. What is one of the most dangerous attitudes prevalent in the world today?

_____

_____

18. What has that attitude caused?

_____

_____

## God's People Have the Answers!

19. Is there anyone on earth who has the answers for the problems of the world that are crashing around us today? If yes, who?

_____

_____

20. What still needs to be done and what should already have been taken care of in those who have the answers?

_____

_____

21. Where do you need to go so that you can be sure to hear Jesus' voice when He says it is time to go home?

_____

_____

22. So many seem to need attention and emotional support right now. Christians, as well as the world, seem to be quite impatient with most of these needy people. What can you do to change that in yourself?

_____

_____

## Attitudes of Compassion

23. What have we all said at times to justify the distancing of ourselves from someone else's need(s)?

_____

_____

_____

_____

24. What do extreme attempts to get attention reveal about a person?

_____

_____

25. To become more understanding, what do we need to do first?

_____

_____

_____

_____

26. What may be the only link someone has to God?

_____

_____

_____

_____

27. What is your understanding of the "baby wrap parable" on pages 191 and 192, and how can you apply it to your life?

_____

_____

_____

_____

## Smaller Area Renewals

28. How do we often block our own healing?

_____

_____

_____

29. What are some of the things the Lord has shown you as truth that you did not see before?

_____

_____

_____

_____

## Binding and Loosing and Healings

30. Do you have any testimonies of healings occuring as a result of using the binding and loosing prayers? Give brief example.

_____
_____
_____
_____

31. In your own words, how would you pray with binding and loosing prayers if you were facing a severe physical problem? Write out prayer here.

_____
_____
_____
_____

How would you pray with these principles for someone else who was very frightened over a disease they had just been diagnosed as having?

_____
_____
_____
_____

## Ungodly Thoughts

32. Why might we cling to critical and judgmental thoughts about others?

_____
_____

33. Some of the suggestions of the enemy are so subtle. Therefore, what can happen in the thought life of the believer who has not been binding his or her mind to the mind of Christ?

_____
_____
_____
_____

34. Some wrong thoughts can become so entrenched in the minds of certain people, they become:

_____
_____

35. Some people become so addicted to wrong thoughts—attitudes, memories, mind-sets—that they continually rerun their old _____ _____ in order to reinforce them.

36. Binding and loosing prayers bring freedom from these old cycles by creating room to
_____ _____ _____ and grace to
_____ and _____ our wounds.

37. We do not have the right to dwell on the unfairness of life or to judge or punish others. What is our responsibility in such an instance?

_____

_____

_____

_____

## Not a Pain-Free Process

38. Living your life according to your own rules is not a pain-free process. True or false?

39. Pain associated with God's workings is always part of what?

_____

_____

_____

_____

40. What is one of the most wonderful things you can finally learn to accept after binding yourself to the steady and fixed things of God?

_____

_____

_____

_____

41. Where does your validation and affirmation come from now? Are you always able to get it without incurring some form of cost? How steady and secure is your present process of receiving validation and affirmation if you happen to fail or don't measure up?

_____

_____

_____

_____

_____

42. What will set you free to walk in new spiritual motivation?

_____

_____

_____

_____

_____

43. What is liable to bring about an all-out, last-ditch attempt of the enemy that will require you to stand firm on what you have come to believe?

_____

_____

_____

44. What do you really need to want in order to follow through and persevere in times of real testing and attack?

_____

_____

## Just Do It!

45. How much of the Greek and Hebrew previously quoted do you need to memorize in order to effectively use the principles of binding and loosing as found in Matthew 16:19?

_____

_____

46. Even if these principles don't make sense to your natural mind, what can you do to begin the process of healing and restoration?

_____

_____

47. Every Scripture you've read and every prayer you've prayed continue to build toward your answers and your victory. But binding and loosing will accomplish what very special thing?

_____

_____

## Changing Lives

48. What can you know is happening when you loose and shatter wrong things in others' lives?

_____

_____

_____

49. As you strip away all that has caused you to oppose your own victory and God's blessings in your life, what does the author say you will become?

_____

_____

_____

_____

# Chapter 10 - Review

**The most significant truths I found in this chapter are:**

1. _____
_____
_____

2. _____
_____
_____

3. _____
_____
_____

4. _____
_____
_____


**I applied these truths to my life as follows:**

1. _____
_____
_____

2. _____
_____
_____

3. _____
_____
_____

4. _____
_____
_____

# Chapter 10 - "Journey" Journal

**Date:**               **Questions I have:**

**Date:**               **Special insights I believe I have learned:**

**Date:**               **Breakthroughs I have experienced:**

# Chapter 10 - Prayer Journal

**Date:**                    **Prayer:**

**Date:**                    **Updates and special encouragements I've received from the Lord:**

**Date:**                    **Answers to prayers:**

**Liberty Savard Ministries**
Mail: P.O. Box 41260
Sacramento, CA 95841

E-mail: liberty@libertysavard.com
Web site: http://www.libertysavard.com

Office: 916-721-7770
Fax: 916-721-8889